Hope in Pain

DShan Berry

BookLeaf Publishing

India | USA | UK

Hope in Pain © 2024 DShan Berry

All rights reserved.

No part of this publication may be reproduced, stored in a retrieval system, or transmitted, in any form or by any means, electronic, mechanical, photocopying, recording or otherwise, without the prior written permission of the presenters.

DShan Berry asserts the moral right to be identified as author of this work.

Presentation by *BookLeaf Publishing*

Web: www.bookleafpub.com

E-mail: info@bookleafpub.com

ISBN: 9789360948917

First edition 2024

For Kristen,

*You've always pointed me back toward hope
no matter the pain I felt. I'm forever
indebted to you and love you, soul sister,
Anam Cara.*

There Hangs a Stillness in my Heart

There hangs a stillness in my heart,
like calm before a gale.
As if my soul, now prescient,
peeks just beyond the Veil.
In these flashes of eternity,
the present moment sighs —
nostalgic for a future not
yet born to you and I.

Post Tenebras Lux

Happiness can follow mourning,
And after darkness, light.
Don't surrender to your struggles;
Resist with all your might.

Like winter wheat relies on frost
To help its seeds to grow,
Tough times can germinate our hearts,
But seem to pass so slow.

May the peace of patience find you,
And ease the pressing ache.
May your spirit reap the harvest
Of joy no one can shake.

Take Heart

We are not the things that haunt us.
We're not the pain we feel.
Two steps up, then one step backward
Is sometimes how we heal.

Though the progress is slow going,
Healthy growth takes time.
Day by day, we're getting closer
To the glorious sublime.

So, take heart, all those who read this,
May these words help you cope:
Light is stronger than the darkness.
May you never give up hope.

Light Through Broken Pieces

My life is a stained glass window —
Light through broken pieces;
My shattered hopes and dreams remade
By the hand of Jesus.

The Son shines through my shards of grief,
Then, jagged edges glow;
His beauty transforms all my pain;
Love putting on a show.

Jesus Wept

"Jesus wept." John 11:35

Jesus wept — His spirit moved from
Seeing His friend's deep grief.
He could have harshly hushed her cries,
Or questioned her belief.

He'd not come for just a visit,
But to ressurect the dead.
But, He did not rebuke her tears;
He joined with them, instead.

The lesson from this shortest verse,
'Bout the Lord upon the throne?
He feels our struggles deeply, and
We never cry alone.

Healed Scars

I used to hide away my scars,
Reminders of my shame;
External signs of inward wounds
Self-injury to blame.

But I can tell the story, now,
With steady hands and voice;
No longer scared to face the truth,
I finally have a choice.

Both acceptance and surrender,
Necessary to heal,
Share a posture of open hands,
Outside of what you feel.

Unmasking the pain takes courage;
Telling your story, too,
Eradicating the stigma
Is something all can do.

Lament

And I have asked a thousand whys
And shook my fist at God.
I've wept, alone, a million tears
Behind a stark facade.

I've wondered, wand'ring in between
My faith and fear so long,
Have I now started to forget
My sweet Redeemer's song?

Doubts arise despite my knowing,
Despite my faith and hope.
Will I ever stop my questions?
If not, how will I cope?

But in the dark, He shines like stars,
His pin-pricked light, I see.
One day, my tears will be no more,
My heart will be set free.

#Harsh-tags

Counting every letter
Each comma and each space,
But do we count OUR character
When none can see our face?

Tweeting hate is easy,
To lash out through a screen,
But we are called to edify,
Encourage, not demean.

Words can become weapons;
Keystrokes like a guillotine.
Think before you send that tweet.
Say only what you mean.

Be careful what you type.
The words can't be unread.
Even if they get deleted,
They'll live in someone's head.

I pray that things will change
Not for worse, but better.
May my Twitter profile look like
Love lived to the letter.

The Everyday Divine

No voice out of a sunlit sky,
No burning bush for me;
The ruins of a shattered heart
Are where I look for Thee.

For You're near the brokenhearted,
The widows, and the poor;
You bring comfort to those weeping
From mercy in Your stores.

I find You in the whispered hush
Of sighs between my tears.
The Bible says You keep them all,
An off'ring You hold dear.

You manifest Yourself to me
With hugs and notes from friends.
I feel Your warmth in the sunset;
Putting me on the mend.

So, it isn't with much fanfare,
But rather in the still,
You speak unto my fragile soul
Your gentle, perfect will.

Sometimes, I wish for visions, bold,
Or walking on the sea,
But You're still in the everyday
And simple folks like me.

Blue Christmas

With red and green surrounding me,
All I can feel is blue.
The music of the caroling
Does not seem to ring true.

The darker, shorter days inch by,
Stealing my joy and mirth.
It's hard to want to celebrate
This Christmas here on Earth.

But, a Light shines in the darkness,
Like the Star, long ago,
To guide our souls to Him
Who will make all things whole.

He came helpless, as a baby,
Died of His own free will
Upon the cross for all our sins.
The scars He carries, still.

So, take heart this Christmas season,
Though the winter might seem bleak.
There's hope in the arms of Jesus,
Whom wise people still seek.

Atomic Advice

Like the atoms in everything,
We're infinitesimally small,
And yet infinitely needed
So things don't stop or stall.

Like them, you are essential;
You hold a sacred space.
There's none can fill it quite like you.
No one could take your place.

Remember that each time you think,
"I am not needed here."
You're not a burden to be borne.
You're precious, and you're dear.

Best Friend

The sorrow aches a little less,
When I am by your side.
Your presence feels like coming home,
A sacred place to hide.

Understanding all my silence,
You're patient for my speech;
Your love — real, and warm, and freeing —
Never out of reach.

The light you shine into my life
Helps keep the dark at bay.
You're ever pointing me to hope
In all you do and say.

Covered

Though darkness surrounds me, it bears not
death's sting,
'Tis but the shadow under Your wing.

Hidden in your love, here, I am found,
Freed from the shame which had kept me bound.

Jesus, the Rock to which I can cling.
Covered by mercy, Your praises I sing.

You beckon me closer to your side,
Where my pain's transformed, my spirit revived.

My soul is awash in tides of peace.
Redeemed! Restored! My heart, released!

The Shadows of the Clouds

The shadows of the clouds
Slide slant among the hills.
They drift across my aching heart
And echo how I feel.

I know this darkness comes
To pass and not to stay,
But, always, there's a part of me
Which feels I've been betrayed

But God's back isn't turned;
He weeps along with me
And holds me in His strong, right hand.
Someday, I will be free.

Questions

I sometimes wonder who I'd be
Had I a different family.

What would I say, what would I think?
Would I like blue or favor pink?

What language would come from my mouth?
Would I live West or in the South?

What kind of jokes would tickle me,
And what perspectives would I see?

What sort of stories would I tell?
Of mountaintops or ocean swells?

What kind of music would I hear,
And would I hold the same things dear?

What history would be my own?
Would I feel different in my bones?

I'll never know with certainty,
So, I guess I'll just be me.

Branded by Miracles

I'm forever branded by miracles —
First, my name, then the scar on my chest.
Both stories tell of God's power divine,
How His goodness and mercy don't rest.

My mom nearly died while pregnant with me
And we suffered the loss of my twin.
It seemed things were going from bad to worse
'Til they began asking God to break in.

The doctor — inspired — tried one last thing,
It saved both my life and my mother's.
She took his last name and made it my first.
I remember each time I tell others.

The scar on my chest came when I was three —
My ribcage, malformed, needed mending.
As the surgeon repaired me, my heart stopped
Which could have sent me to my ending.

Once again, people prayed for my healing.
Once again, the Lord's healing came through.
My heart started beating with life once more;
I'm living proof of miracles true.

Love Wins

Diamonds are beautiful,
pure, sparkling,
yet tough.

Graphite is dark,
brittle, easily transferred,
and fragile.

Diamonds outlast graphite
no contest, but,
fundamentally,
they come from the same place — carbon.

The difference lies
in how they respond
to heat and pressure.

Simple carbon must
patiently endure much,
with perseverance,
to become something enduring.

Graphite forms
more quickly and easily,
but doesn't stay.

Like diamonds and graphite,
love and hate
have the same source —
our hearts.

The world
and how
we respond to it
shapes our hearts.

If we take the easy way,
the path of least resistance,
hate and bitterness
will make us graphite,

but, if we are willing
to put up the good fight,
and persist by choosing
to respond in love,
we can shine like diamonds.

Yes, hate leaves it's marks
on the world,
but, like a pencil,
with time and care
it can, ultimately, be erased.

Love etches itself

on the world, forever.
Love lasts.
Love wins.

Hope in Pain

"There may not always be a cure, but there is
always healing."
   — Deany Laliotis

There may not always be a cure,
But there's always healing.
No less than the Truth is needed
When life sends us reeling.

Although we may not understand;
Trust His ways are higher.
He's righteous love forever;
He cannot be a liar.

By a Thread

Barely hanging on by a thread,
I reached for Jesus' hem.
Resources all spent and empty,
My hope had almost dimmed.

But, my faith told me my healing
Was almost in my grasp,
Even though, in my time waiting,
Almost twelve years had passed.

Ever aware of my unclean state,
I willingly risked scorn.
If I remained unhealed that day,
My heart would have been torn.

But when he called out, "Who touched me?"
His voice, tender and clear,
I somehow knew that, with this man,
I had nothing to fear.

Instantly, He'd healed my body;
My wound had ceased its flow.
And, now, He stood in front of me.
Humbled, I knelt down, low.

Then, He said my faith had healed me,
And I could go in peace.
A weight lifted off my shoulders.
At last, I felt released.

Help My Unbelief

Lord, help my unbelief!
I cry aloud once more.
I'm begging for relief —
Curled, fetal, on the floor.

The truth rings hollow here
In this place of sorrow,
Surrounded by my fears,
Dreading my tomorrow,

Facing all this darkness,
I wish I could forget
The pain of yesterday,
And all of my regrets,

But this hope still abides —
God sits with those in grief.
He's weeping by my side.
This helps my unbelief.

Offering

Mere words are all I have to give,
But what I have, I offer.
Like the widow from the Bible,
I'll place two mites in the coffer.

That offering, so miniscule
By all the standards of the day,
Is how I feel about my words,
As though I haven't much to say.

May I speak of Truth and Beauty,
And Love flow freely from my pen.
May Hope echo in my poems
To comfort all who hurt within.

Though these offerings are meager,
I humbly lay them at Your feet.
Please, bless my work and craftsmanship
Until my journey is complete.